Leadership Secrets The Other Books Won't Tell You

A New Leader's Guide

Lieutenant Commander
Charles "Chip" Lutz
United States Navy, Retired

Leadership Secrets The Other Books Won't Tell You
A New Leader's Guide

ISBN-13: 978-1500339975
ISBN-10: 1500339970

Cover and Interior Design by Abigayle Lutz

If want others to follow, GO FIRST!

The BIG Secret!

What's the secret to leading people? The answer is that there is no secret. I've stood at the bookstore (like you), dumbfounded, by all of the titles that were in front of me on the subject of leadership. Each one seemed to purport that the author had, in fact, been made privy to the intangible secrets to effective leadership through the most curious of paths. There were secrets that came from Santa, Squirrels, Jesus, several dead presidents and yet a few others. So MANY secrets!!

While contemplating all of the choices, I couldn't help but think back to when I was a junior Sailor and worked for Captain Pat. Captain Pat was (quite possibly) the most personable leader that I've ever worked for. On more than one occasion I got to spend some "one on one" time with him as his driver. While taking him to a meeting one day, I asked, "Captain, how did you make to where you are? What's the secret to being a good leader?" He laughed (as he always did) and responded,

> **"Lutzey, my boy, there is no secret. Take care of your people and they'll take care of you. Leadership is all about the people."**

In life we get a lot of advice. Some good, some bad, and even more that we neither asked for nor wanted. That day, I asked for it and I got it! People, became the cornerstone of how I led. To me, there aren't any "natural born" leaders. Some have charisma (from the Greek word for "divinely inspired gift") that make us want to follow but, as Captain Pat said, there is no secret...leadership is all about the people and is a deliberative process. It would be nice if there were a "cookie cutter" method that worked for everyone, but the path to leading them is as varied as the people involved.

? **What's the BIG SECRET!?**
The only secret to leading people is that it's all about people!

The "Not So Glorious" Secret

Looks like you've made it! Hooray! You've been put in charge and now all eyes are on you to move the team forward! WHAT!? Or, you're contemplating taking on a leadership role and you want to do your best. Either way, I'm glad you've gotten this book. As I was "growing up" as a leader, there were plenty of people around to give me advice. Some advice was good, some was not so good and a lot was just plain bad. Some of the best advice came from my brother, Matt, just prior to my joining the Navy and is the first advice I'd like to pass to you as you contemplate jumping into a new leadership role. Are you ready for it? Here it is: Leading ain't no birthday party! My brother, Matt's, advice was actually "boot camp isn't a birthday party." (This advice came from him when I asked him what to expect when I went to boot camp).

I want to pass that same sage, brotherly advice along to everyone when they ask me if they should take a leadership role. I want to tell them simply, "Well, it's not a birthday party!" That's the "Not so Glorious" secret about leading. I think we have a tendency to romanticize the leadership role. Don't get me wrong, leading is rewarding and is also what I love to do but it's not all cake, ice cream, and presents. Why? Because leading is about people and people are messy. As great as getting the opportunity to lead is, potential leaders need to ask themselves some serious questions as they contemplate taking the next step. Contemplate these:

Am I ready to make unpopular decisions? Sometimes, doing what is right makes people angry. Not every decision will be well received or liked.

Am I ready to put others before myself? Leading is about serving. The needs of the team come before your own needs.

Am I ready to not be liked? Some won't like the fact that you're in that position instead of them. Others, won't like the donuts you bring in.

Am I ready to pass all of the credit and take all of the blame? As leader, your team's success is theirs and their failure, is yours. You can delegate authority but not responsibility. The buck stops with you!

Am I ready to be on the "they" team? No matter how much you empathize with the team, you're the "they" that gets bitched about around the water cooler (and to their spouse).

Can I stand up for what is right in the face of adversity? Whether it's with your team or your superiors, leaders must stand up for what they believe in. No flip flops or milk toast allowed.

Can I confront a situation in person? It may be giving bad news, correcting problem behavior or having to let someone go. Regardless, giving the news in person is the only way to go. Email confrontations are for managers, not leaders.

Do I like repeating myself? No matter how much you communicate, there will be those who don't listen. No matter how many times you say it, you'll need to say it again.

Can I laugh at myself? Leaders who can laugh at themselves help create an atmosphere of risk without fear of reprise. If you take yourself too seriously, people will be laughing AT you and not with you.

Can I walk the talk? If you are saying one thing and doing another, your team will be the first to notice and will follow suit.

Am I ready to know even when I don't know? In a stressful situation that seems to have no apparent solution, teams need to know that you know what to do (even when you don't know). Keep your insecurities and your stress to yourself, it will only complicate the situation.

If you can answer "YES!" to these questions then, absolutely, you should seek out the first leadership position that comes along. If not, can you answer "YES" to this question:

> **DO I WANT TO MAKE A LASTING DIFFERENCE FOR OTHERS?**

If you can answer "yes" to that one then you can weather all the other hardships of leading messy people. A strong desire to make a difference can trump everything else. Just remember that there are no "one size fits all" or "cookie cutter" solutions to leading a team. There will be good parts, bad parts and fun parts but it has to be experienced for yourself.

> ?
>
> **What's the BIG SECRET!?**
> Leading isn't a Birthday Party but if you can say "YES" to making a difference, you are ready!

The Secret About Leadership "Boot camps"

Just like you can't read ONE book and be the best leader around, you also can't spend one day training and achieve that same result. Boot-camp is real but leadership boot-camps are a farce. Here is what a real boot-camp is like…

Sweat poured from every pore in my body and I struggled to keep my legs "six inches off the deck" during an intensive physically training session at boot camp. The company commander (a Navy version of a Drill Instructor) stood powerfully over all of the recruits yelling:

"On your backs!"

"On your bellies!"

"Flutter kicks"

"Push up position…HOLD IT….HOLD IT!"

Moans and groans came from every corner of the room as this "punishment" seemed to last forever. Then, with a smirk, the Company Commander yelled; "Are you tired yet!?"

In unison, we all yelled, "YES SIR!"

"I'm not!" He replied as he calmly took a swig of his coffee. "We're gonna make these walls sweat, recruits!"

That, my friends, is a small glimpse of what goes on in an actual boot camp. For those of you who have served and experienced the same, I salute you. It is what we call, sociologically, a "total institution socialization." A breaking down of people to get them to conform and behave in a certain manner.

That is why when I hear the term "boot camp" attached to a weekend marketing scheme to get people to become better leaders, I cringe. The thought that you can go away for a day or a weekend to what is referred to as a "boot-camp" is ill titled and nothing AT ALL like boot-camp. What most leaders need is a re-boot and not a boot camp.

Like I stated previously, leadership is a deliberative process. There is no "one size fits all" method to it and most of it (since it is individualized for leader and follower) is trial and error. It is finding the fit of what works for you and your people to get the job done. A reboot helps you do this. Take some time to find out how to get along, get connected, and learn to employ basic human relations as a strategy to engage your team.

For information on my re-boot program, email me!

> ?
> **What's the BIG SECRET!?**
> Most leaders don't need a "Bootcamp" as much as they need a re-boot on how to get along with people!

The Secret About Assumption Errors

I had a supervisor, Dave, that knew when he told me I couldn't do something, I'd work even harder to prove that I could do it. He was a great supervisor. It was easy for him to motivate me because we were cut from the same cloth. That was lucky for Dave and it worked. Most new leaders fall into the trap of making the same critical assumption errors as Dave. Sometimes it works, sometimes not. What are the assumption errors?

- We assume people like what we like (motivation, rewards, etc).
- We assume people know what we know.
- We assume people know how well they are doing.

How do we combat making these critical assumption errors?

Stop, ask, and tell.

Stop what you're doing and take a moment to talk to your people.

Ask them what motivates them. Ask them what says "reward" to them and listen! Ask them if they understand what it is they're doing and how they fit in.

Tell them how they're doing. Not only what they are doing well but also what they can improve upon.

It is easy to motivate when your team is just like you, however, that's rarely the case in today's increasingly diverse workplace. Stopping, asking, and telling will help you leverage the best asset you have....your people.

> ?
> **What's the BIG SECRET!?**
> Don't assume anything! Stop, ask and TELL people how well they do!

The Secret About Finding Your Center

Lastly, find your center. You're unique and that's what makes you a unique, different, and an Unconventional Leader.

We all come from someplace. It's our roots and routes that shape us; our roots, where we come from and our routes, those intersections of life that make an impact on how we see the world. For me, I learned a lot just growing up a "husky" (fat) kid. One such example comes from gym class back in high school.

Fall, 1982...The basketball tipped off the top of John's fingers and, seemingly in slow motion, arced high up in the air and descended down into my chubby little hands. WHAT!? I had the ball!? I looked up, ball in hand, as a pack of much taller, athletic classmates ran to surround me (as a pack of ravenous wolves would surround a pug with a piece of meat). Surrounded, outnumbered, short, and never having had the ball before, I panicked and yelled, "BACK UP! My contact just popped out!" Immediately, the crowd stepped back and started looking down to see it. Now, completely open, I turned and took the shot to make the basket. The ball hurled skyward (again, seemingly in slow motion) and, anti-climatically, completely missed the basket. Then, astutely, one person yelled, "Hey! He doesn't wear contacts!"

Yes, I grew up a short, fat kid. It was my own fault. I don't blame it on genetics or anything else…I just liked to eat! Truthfully, I never met a donut I didn't like. And, although I wasn't athletic and hated team sports, those years as a fat kid taught me a lot about how to look at life, connect with people, and lead more effectively. Here are just a few tasty nuggets of sugar laden wisdom I can share on what growing up with girth teaches.

Industry

Let's face it; it's a pretty person's world. I don't make the rules, I (like everyone else) just have to live by them. Everyone has to work hard to succeed, but those with any kind of social "stigma" (like weight) have to work even harder to move forward. Being a fat kid taught me how to work hard, think on my feet and not be afraid to take the shot – that, even if some maneuvering was needed to shoot, it was always better to take the shot and miss than wish you had. That's what we, as leaders, need to do as well, isn't it and what is needed in today's world? That we work hard and make decisions? Granted, not every decision is going to be right or popular, but our people count on us to put in the time and respond to issues. Even if we miss the shot, credibility is gained through action not just talking a good game.

Loyalty

My brother, Matt, says that if someone "pats me on the head once, I am their friend for life." This extreme loyalty emerged from forging strong bonds with the people that meant the most in my life – those that would look past the fluffy exterior of "me as a fat kid" and take the time to find out who I really was. That learned loyalty impacted my ability to serve my country and those around me with truth, honesty, and unwavering tenacity. That's what we all want in a leader! Someone who knows us, knows our capabilities, and has our "back" when situations get tough or mistakes are made. That's what anyone that ever worked with me knew to expect and what your people should expect as well. You, as leader, are the buffer! You need to have their backs and fight until the end to support the team and the cause. Your loyalty to those you serve is key in building community!

Humility.

Any fat kid who has had to be on the "skins" team knows humility! That, coupled with the social awkwardness of just being a teenager, gave me an ability to laugh at situations that would have otherwise made one cry. Even when I "lost my contact" and took the shot, the silliness of the situation made my other classmates laugh and eased the fact I had missed the shot. As a leader, this ability to make a joke or make light of a situation (even in the most difficult of times) eased the stress of the situation for everyone around me. As a result, our teams were more creative, productive, and enjoyed a greater cohesiveness. Had I stressed them out, the opposite would have been true. Forgetting your position, working alongside people, and losing the ego eases everyone's burden. Laugh often – it's the quickest way to connect with others.

Although I was a fat kid, I think growing up is challenging for everyone – we all face challenges, are self-conscious, and worry about fitting in. To this day, I still can't play basketball and I still love donuts but I wouldn't change anything about my childhood. The lessons I learned in the jungles of middle school as a fat kid helped me learn to connect better, work harder and lead more effectively.

? **What's the BIG SECRET!?**
Knowing your center helps you lead authentically and what makes you unique (and memorable)!

The Secret Of What To Keep To Yourself

"Nooooooo! Please do not share ANYTHING else with me!" is what I thought as she droned on about everything that was going on in her life.

As a new Officer in the Navy, I worked for a Lieutenant named, Sheila. She was nice, however, didn't know what to keep to herself. It was then that I learned that there is a LOT of truth to the saying, "familiarity breeds contempt." In that, the more she talked (and I knew about the intimate details of her life), the less I respected her.

There's a fine line we walk, as leaders, in sharing enough to be personable and be seen as human and too much that we lose the respect of our people. That line is different for every leader and every relationship, however, I think there are some things that we should never share.

1. **Gossip**. Don't engage in he said, she said, what you make, what others make, who is sleeping with who, or how sexy you think the person down in accounting is. We all love a little gossip (I know I do) and it is fun to blather on about how Billy jilted Suzy and how Suzy got back at him by pulling a "Fatal Attraction" like move but idle gossip degrades the trust between all involved.

2. **Details of your sex life.** It is GREAT that your spouse, boyfriend, girlfriend and/or "buddy" brings new meaning to the Rick James song, "Super Freak." Some might be jealous to hear about it and some might be repulsed. Regardless, all will get a visual of you that they don't need (or want). Do EVERYONE a favor and keep it to yourself.

3. **Personal problems.** Yes, it is sad that your kids are in/out of jail and that your parents moved without giving a forwarding address. However, your people aren't your therapists and they'll start wondering why (with so many problems) you are in charge of them. Tell your bartender about it (unless you manage a bar).

4. **Discipline of others.** Yes, you really showed Johnny who was "boss" when you docked him pay, gave him a letter of reprimand, and took away his birthday but Johnny still works there and doesn't need anyone else to know.

5. **Politics or Religion.** If you are a Senator or a Priest, disregard this and share either with those around you (politicians can use some religion and clergy can use some politics). In today's increasingly diverse world, no one should feel pressured to believe what you believe or vote how you vote. Put the bumper sticker on your car to show your support for your candidate and be respectful of others.

6. **Bodily fluids.** Office romances are never a good idea and can end up with a visit to Human Resources.

Like I stated, every workplace and work relationship is different. I am an advocate for connecting with the people that work for you and knowing them as people. I am also an advocate for leaders being seen as human. That requires some disclosure and risk on a leaders part. But, there are some things that you should just keep to yourself so that you can keep the respect of your people.

> **?**
> **What's the BIG SECRET!?**
> Share enough with your team that they know you but not so much that they lose respect for you!

The Secret Of Establishing Your Authority

I was a 30 year old, young, Lieutenant who had just volunteered to be in charge of a 300 person security department. Uncle Charlie (whose name has been changed to protect the innocent) was a seasoned Police Officer with over 30 years on the job and one of my Precinct Commanders (I had three Precincts). When he asked to meet with me, I knew what it was about. I had heard through the grapevine that he wasn't very happy to be working for me.

Many times, as leaders, we are thrust into a position of authority ahead of people who may be as qualified, over qualified, or more experienced on the job than we are. Regardless of any of those qualifiers, you (as I was) were chosen to be put in that position for a reason. You can't question that reason or your qualifications. You need to establish your authority early on or it will be questioned by your people, consistently. Here's how I handled Uncle Charlie:

I established early on my authority by "marking" the territory. When Uncle Charlie came to my office, he came "packing" (yes, he had a gun but that's not what I'm referring to). He was prepared. He had all of the rules from the Office of Personnel Management on how his civilian pay grade was senior to mine as an Officer in the Navy. I listened to what he had to say, acknowledged it and the and then explained how things were; that my commission was tendered by the President of the United States and that overruled the guidelines he laid out. I had been put in this position for a reason and, however much I appreciated the chart he showed me, I was in charge and expected him to recognize it, accept it, and help. He left knowing that I wanted to work together and I that I needed his experience for the TEAM to be successful.

I remained in charge. I think one of the most important rules of establishing your authority is that, *if you want others to follow, go first.* If it's hard, dangerous, arduous, meticulous, or tiresome, you must go first. You can't have followers unless you are leading. Leading requires going first. I went first in all things (with Uncle Charlie and others). I even went first during Pepper Spray training (I think they gave me an extra shot in the eyes just to try and humble me a bit). Figure out what needs to be done and set the pace from the front.

I made decisions. I like to use the term collaborative direction. When making decisions, I like to get the input from the team but, in many cases, the decision (and the ramifications) lied solely with me and I needed to direct my decision in the best interest of the organization. In the times that no one knew what to do I, as leader, had to know what to do. I went to Uncle Charlie for many things and asked his advice. In a way, I think he felt like he was mentoring me so that the TEAM would do well. When decisions were bad, I took the heat. When they were great, I shared the wealth. Use your team to get all the info you need to make the decision but make it and then live with it.

I gave power away. If there was something that needed me to be involved, I was involved. If not, I gave the power to the lowest that it could be. The only person that can bestow power is the person with the power. I gave Uncle Charlie a lot more latitude to make a difference than he had with my predecessor. If he needed me, I was there. If he needed a buffer during a fall out, I buffed. Find out where power can be given and let people go. You'll be surprised on what they'll get done (and the places you'll go).

It wasn't the easiest two years working with Uncle Charlie but, when I was transferring, he let me know he was going to miss working for me. I couldn't have accomplished what I needed to without Uncle Charlie and he couldn't have done what he needed to without me. In the end, I respected his experience and he respected my authority.

> ?
>
> **What's the BIG SECRET!?**
> Leading is NOT for the faint at heart. It takes intestinal fortitude to mark that territory and give power away but it has to be done.

The Secret Of Recovering From A HUGE Blunder

Back in the olden days, when dinosaurs roamed the earth and thoughts were kept on "post-its" (and not a smart phone), I was in charge of the travel budget for my squadron. Since we had planes, travel was part of what we did and keeping a tight budget was paramount in our ability to make things "go."

When I took over as the travel clerk, I had taken the time to move us out of the dark, dark ages of tracking funds on an abacus and stone to a new thing called a "Spreadsheet." It was an amazing tool that helped me keep the budget balanced easily. I had been using this tool successfully for about a year when the comptroller called me and told me I was out of money. Being a tad cocky, I argued that this was impossible because I showed money on my spreadsheet and that, invariably, she was wrong. This didn't go over very well. To prove my rightness, I went through my entire year's expenditures...line by line and found that I was the one that was wrong. Somewhere, tucked away in cell, a formula was missing and I was in the hole....BIG! To make matters worse, we had a big mission coming up and I had just briefed my boss that we were A-OK on funds...all systems were GO! I was beside myself with grief.

How could I have missed something so simple? How could I be the one responsible for us not making mission? What was I going to do?

Yes, my friends, I Blundered with a Capital B! It wasn't the first time in my life and it hasn't been the last. We all mess up, slip up and trip up from time to time. I handled this time just like how, as a leader, I like people to come to me after a blunder has been discovered.

First, I admitted it. My first instinct was that of survival. This was a big mistake and I was sure I was going to get a major chewing out. I went to my boss and let him know what was going on. He was upset but appreciated my honesty. Few can argue with you when you admit you're wrong and made a mistake. His anger was tempered when I didn't expect him to correct it. I left letting him know that I was "on it."

I got out in front of it. In this instance, I immediately called the comptroller and let her know what was going on and asked what I could do. Every problem has some kind of solution - even if it's unsolvable, it is sometimes still workable. The comptroller explained to me that out of money is out of money BUT we could borrow from the next quarter. If you've blundered big, bring others together (if you can) to help you try and get to a solution.

I went to my boss with a solution. No one wants more work on their plate (your boss included). My mistake was his mistake and if I didn't correct it, he'd have to. He was used to this from me. Not only did I screw the pooch regularly, I also would have solutions for fixing it (part of the reason he felt better when I told him I was "on it" when I told him about the mistake).

No one is perfect and we all make mistakes. The difference comes down to what we do AFTER the mistake is made. We can hide it, hope that no one ever finds out, blame it on something (or someone else) or we can jump into the fire and fix it. As a leader, I expect people to make mistakes. It is part of the learning process. However, I love those people that come to me with the solution to fix the mistake. Those are the people who won't make that mistake again and, in the end, will help the team grow. So, don't worry about slipping up, tripping up, or messing up....as long as you know how to handle it afterwards.

? **What's the BIG SECRET!?**
Own your mistakes and be part of the solution!

The Secret Of Getting Over Your Fears

I'm not afraid of the Boogie Man, but I have watched enough episodes of "Snapped" on The Oxygen Channel to make me a tad fearful when my wife, Gwen, gives me the crazy eyes. Fear is an important emotion. It keeps us from returning the stalkers call. It keeps us alert when we're in the dark alley. It keeps us away from clowns. But, fear, can also keep us from stepping out and taking the risk that we know we should take.

I have as many fear issues as anyone. Having grown up a fat kid, most of my fears stem from the insecurities I learned in the classroom. Those of looking stupid, sounding dumb or not being "good enough." As a leader, those issues still rear their ugly head when I need to do something that is scary and could (if left unattended) stagnate me (and my team) in a pool of "could have been."

How about you? Got a fear demon and need to exorcise it? Here are a few tips I use:

ONE

Quit worrying. "What ifs" are a huge fear for most. Worrying about "What if this?" and "What if that?" are common objections to taking action. Lets set things straight. Worry solves nothing, action does - 95% of what we worry about never happens and the other 5% doesn't matter. And, if you're worried about the accuracy of my statistics....DON'T (I made them up...but find them to be true).

TWO

Stop thinking about the "Why Me?" and start thinking "Why NOT me?" Why shouldn't you be successful? You've done a LOT of great things! You are able to leap tall buildings in a single bound...you were the hero at the big game...you can fit FIVE cheeseburgers in your mouth at one time without choking. Remember those "glory moments" of triumph! Step out of your own way, give yourself a pep talk, and think about the glory of you.

THREE

Own it!. After you quit worrying and get in the right mindset, own your fear and then take a step. If I take one step in the direction of what scares me it, in effect, puts me in control. It also encourages me to take one more step. I'm either going to realize that there's nothing to be scared of or I'm going to walk faster to get the hell out of there. Regardless, I'm in control.

I, like you, have to face the fears of my past all the time. I can either hide under the blankets, suck my thumb, and wait for my mommy to save me OR I can take the risk. There is no reward without risk. Do yourself and your team a favor and quit worrying. Step out...if you do, your team will too (but still stay away from clowns and be weary of the crazy eyes).

?

What's the BIG SECRET!?
95% of what we worry about doesn't happen and the other 5% doesn't matter (and If you're worrying about the accuracy of my percentages, I made them up).

The Secret Of Having The Difficult Conversation

It was a fun job! I was still working my Navy job during the day but started teaching at night. My first semester went off without a hitch. My second, however, proved to be a little bit of a different story. It wasn't bad. It's just that I had a "Chatty Kathy" who kept disrupting the class and talking over me. I had NEVER encountered something like this before. I had taught a lot of classes in the Navy but (even if they weren't interested) people would at least feign interest. Not this guy. I just kept powering through...hoping it would stop. Finally, in the fourth week, I hit my boiling point when he was not only talking but he was also texting and smirking at me. I felt my eye start to twitch as I switched into full Commander Mode. As I opened my mouth to address the situation, what I meant to say (in a very subtle manner) was, "Hey, if you don't want to be here. Please leave." But, what came out of my mouth (in a VERY militant manner) was, "HEY, IF YOU DON'T WANT TO BE HERE....THERE'S THE F#@KING DOOR!" A hush came over the classroom and we ended class shortly thereafter.

There are so many things I did wrong in this situation. Mainly, I didn't have the right conversation with the student when the problem started. I had dealt with many issues like this in the Navy, but, in this new environment, I had forgotten the basics of how to have a potentially contentious conversation with people that irritate me. Do you have a person you need to address and are afraid that emotion might overtake you until you bludgeon them with a blunt object? Here's how to handle it so you don't "pull a Chip":

First, address it early. Much like when you ignore when a child takes five cookies instead of one, it becomes the accepted norm. Ignoring problem behavior makes it acceptable behavior. As soon as a problem behavior rears up, take the person aside and let him know what the expectation is.

Second, start with a question" I find asking a question first gives the person an opportunity to be heard and makes them feel less defensive. In my case, I could have asked my student, "What do you want to get out of this class?" That question wouldn't have made him feel attacked and would have led to a good conversation on how to get there together.

Third, listen to what the person is saying. Nod your head, make eye contact, and repeat back for understanding. Easy enough, right? NO! Most of the time we're wanting to be heard first. We're trying to listen but all we're really thinking about is how irritated we are and what needs to be said next. Think about that stuff before or after the conversation but not now...actually listen.

Lastly, lead the conversation where you want it to go. Again, I use questions to include the person. I might use, "What do you think about this?" Or, "How do you think we can do that?" With my student, I should have (after asking the first question and listening) asked, "Do you think we can work on...." instead of what I said..."GET OUT!"

Hindsight is 20/20. Like I stated, these are things I knew how to do in leading people in the Navy but, in a new environment, I had forgotten some basics. I still came out okay, though. Most of the other students thanked me because they were tired of his distractions and the Dean understood (once I apologized and explained the situation). The rest of us powered through the remainder of the semester and had a good time. I say the "rest of us" because my problem student never came back after my explosion. I lost one because I let my emotions rule over logic.

?

What's the BIG SECRET!?
Most of us are wanting to be heard first when we should be setting the expectation and listening.

The Secret To making The Right (Ethical) Decision

I was certainly at an impasse. I wanted our team to do well on the inspection, however, I wasn't comfortable doing what my supervisor suggested. Instead of just telling the inspectors what was wrong and taking the "discrepancy", he suggested that I "misrepresent" the paperwork to make it look like it was in compliance.

Does this sound familiar? Are you torn between two ethical choices? Feeling like a tool? When something seems amiss, it usually is. When I'm pushed, I go through this process to determine what the right course is.

First, I seek my moral compass. Inherently, I know what's right and what's not. If it feels bad...there is usually a reason. Go with your gut on what is right and power through. I think most people have this compass and do (can) use this method.

Second, I think about what my Mom would say about it. Let's face it, moms know what's wrong and what's not. Further, they aren't shy about giving you the "look" when you did something you shouldn't have. This, however, goes with the assumption that your Mom isn't Lizzie Borden, Bloody Mary, or any of the other women on the "10 Most Evil Women in History" list. If they are, you can ask my mom (she'd be happy to not only tell you what to do, she'll Skype you to give you a disapproving eye).

Last, I think of how this would look to others if they knew. Mainly, would I want this on Facebook...published to all my "friends" (I put friends in quotations because, honestly, I don't know who half of the people are). Yes, peer pressuring myself into compliance, if necessary.

On this occasion, I stuck with my moral compass (which is my norm) and told the inspectors what was wrong. They appreciated my honesty and helped me correct the problem (without issue) and we didn't get hurt for it during the inspection. Most people appreciate honesty and you can't be faulted for doing what is right.

But, if you are penalized and do get in trouble for doing what is right, at least you can rest easy knowing you acted ethically.

? **What's the BIG SECRET!?**
Follow your moral compass. If it doesn't feel right, don't do it.

The Secret To Picking Your Team

Oh, sweatpants, how do I love thee? Let me count the ways! I love your comfort. I love your flexibility. I love the way you let me be free and how you never seem to get dirty (no matter how long I wear you). I don't, however, like how you lie to me.

When first retiring from the Navy, I traded my Khaki uniform for a new "sweatpants uniform." For two months, as I wrote, called, and created new things for my business, I had a steady rotation of three pairs of sweatpants to wear. I loved them and they loved me. In that two months, my sweatpants told me it was okay to eat as much as I wanted because, they, still fit. Then, suddenly, it was time to go out and meet the world as a civilian and when I went to put on my old custom tailored suit, it didn't fit. No matter how much

I rolled around on the bed (and I was rolling), trying to fasten my pants, I couldn't get them together. Actually, it was amazing that I even got the pants over my big butt. My sweatpants, however comfortable and loving they had been, had lied to me about the weight I had gained.

I've found the same thing to be true with teams I've been on. Many team members are like sweatpants. They are comfortable! I love them! They allow me to be free! But, they too..lie to me. After a while when it's time to venture out, I find myself wholly unprepared to face the realities of what's out there because I've just gotten too comfortable. All wardrobes need some diversity! Building a team? Here are the wardrobe articles YOU NEED:

The Shorts: Shorts are fun! Shorts are casual! Shorts keep things light and active! They know how to have fun and get things done.

The Dress Pants: Dress pants keep it formal! They remind you that there's more than comfort and fun. Dress pants keep you on the straight and narrow (and out of jail).

The Jeans: Jeans are heavy workers. They are broken in and, no matter how battered and dirty they get, they are ready for more wear. Jeans don't care about what they look like, they just want to get stuff done.

The Tight Pants: These are the pants that fit you two years ago. They remember how things used to be when you were in shape and urge you to get back on track in doing things right. You might not go to them all the time (because they're so uncomfortable), but you know you need to keep them.

And...yes....

The Sweat Pants: They may lie to you and tell you you're not getting fat, however, they just make life a bit sweeter and you ARE REALLY comfortable with them.

Just like having all sweatpants in your wardrobe, having all of any one of these types on your team is a recipe for disaster. Diversity brings depth. Diversity brings breadth! Don't get caught with your pants down! Build your team with more than sweatpants. You'll always be ready for any occasion.

> ? **What's the BIG SECRET!?**
> You need more than one type of person on your team just like you need more than one type of pants to wear. And, yes, sweatpants lie to you.

The Secret To Making It Through The Office Social Intact

Yes, it's that time...TIME FOR THE ANNUAL OFFICE PARTY! WOOT WOOT! You've been waiting, patiently, for it to come up and now, finally, it is here. That person in accounting has been giving you the "flirty eye" and you are ready to go for the gold!

Last year the party was legendary! You got hired and started work a couple of days too late and missed it all. You did, however, hear about the exploits of Jimmy. Jimmy was the life of the party. He drank everyone under the table....he conversed with nearly everyone there....he showed "no mercy' with the ladies...and he even let the boss know what the culture was REALLY like. Jimmy is a maverick! Jimmy is a ladies man! Jimmy knows how to party! Jimmy.....is no longer is with the company. Such a shame...he, surely, would've made things really fun this year.

Jimmy, obviously, had a little too much fun last year. His antics got the best of him and now, Jimmy, is no longer with the company. How do you make the most of the event of the year and not be like Jimmy?

Strategy One

Don't drink. Now, don't get me wrong. I like my Vodka Tonics. I feel they cleanse the soul and make most things bearable, however, this is an event you should think moderation. Remember that time you and your friends drank so much you woke up in a strange place, wearing someone else's underwear? Yeah....that's a great story. But, it's not the story you want to tell on Monday (especially if you're wearing your boss's underwear).

Strategy Two

Don't engage in conversation about politics or religion.

Aren't you thankful that your Mom took you to church and "learned you up" about all things God? NEWS FLASH.....your mom isn't at the party and the person India, doesn't think your Christmas tradition of London Broil is as cool as you do.

Further, your boss is an avid supporter of the people you DIDN'T vote for last year (and, yet, you still have the bumper sticker on your car). As a rule of thumb....stay away from anything that is potentially combustible.

Strategy Three

Don't wear your "Beer drinkers make better lovers" or "Honk if you're horny" T-shirts. Sure, they're great conversations pieces.....in the unemployment line. Dress like you're going to see Mom in the hospital.

Strategy Four

Have a great joke or funny story to share. Just make sure it's not the story about you waking up after binge drinking in a strange place in someone else's underwear...or about someone in the room. Make it about you. Self deprecating humor is a great way to show how humble and lovable you are. Unless you say something completely inappropriate, no one will remember what you said, they'll only remember how you made them feel (warm, fuzzy, and happy).

Strategy Five

Stay away from the person from accounting. Yes, you've been getting the "flirty eye" but this isn't the time (or place) to start the office romance. *NOTE: I think office romances are a bad idea in any case (they never turn out well).* Wait to ask the person out until after the party. Go on a REAL date (after the party) away from all the co-workers who will gossip about things that didn't even happen (which may make you sound cooler than you are but will, ultimately, tarnish your reputation).

Strategy Six

Leave early (especially if you supervise anyone). Don't push to be the last drunk standing. If you supervise, leave early so your people don't have you witness them as the last drunk standing. You can catch up on what happened on Monday.

Strategy Seven

Leave with who you came with. I don't think this needs any explanation (especially if you're married).

This is going to be an AWESOME party! It will be EPIC! Everyone will be talking about it for months....with or without you! Stick to the plan and they'll be talking about it with you and NOT ABOUT YOU! Afterwards, give Jimmy a call. I'm sure he'd love to hear how it went.

?

What's the BIG SECRET!?
Think ahead and keep it professional at the office social. It's better to have less fun than to be unemployed.

The Secret Of How To Deal With the Bad Apple

Let's face it, we can pick our nose but we can't all pick our teams. It would be great to be able to "Kingdom Build," (as my old boss would say) but, sometimes, we get a legacy team...one that has been around, has a way of doing things, and is set in their ways. Ninety percent of the people on that team may be GREAT but, undoubtedly, you'll get one or two "bad apples." It could be their negativity, lack of work ethic, or sarcastic nature that makes them rotten to work with. Regardless, the entire team feels the effect and is brought down as a result. You've tried talking, reasoning, and counseling...what's a leader to do?

I'm glad you asked! I love B. F. Skinner and his theories on operant conditioning because, for me, they just make sense in trying to change behavior of people. Skinner coined the term operant conditioning; it means roughly the changing of behavior with reinforcement which is given after the desired response. If you have behaviors you want to change, I believe that the entire office is a Skinner Box and you're the scientist that can get what he wants if you use the right reinforcers. Here's how to deal with that bad apple using Skinner as a guide.

OPTION ONE

Reinforce the behavior you want to see with a reward (thereby trying shape the behavior into one you want to see again). Let's say ,Billy (our bad apple), actually says something positive at a meeting. That's when you would stop, acknowledge it, and say what a good idea it was. Or, Billy is constantly late on getting his reports in. One day, out of the blue, he turns in his reports early and you give him a piece of candy corn. Do this often enough and the behavior you want to see will be the one repeated more often.

OPTION TWO

Make Billy's work life uncomfortable until he shows the behavior you want to see. This would be a good example of negative reinforcement (the removal of an unpleasant reinforcer when the desired behavior is given). Let's go back to Billy's reports. Billy is still late on his reports and you REALLY need him to get them done on time. To help this along, you visit him every 30 minutes to ask how it is going and when he'll have them done. Besides being extreme micro-managing, this is going to be a constant unpleasant experience for BIlly (not only because he hates it but also because your breath smells from the fish tacos you ate at lunch). When Billy gets his reports in on time, you go away, the uncomfortable pressure is removed, Billy feels relieved, and Billy repeats the behavior of getting his reports done on time..

OPTION THREE

You can punish Billy. Punishment is a little different from reinforcing behaviors because it is used eliminate a response rather than increase it. Let's not return to Billy's reports but go back to the meeting where Billy was at. Let's say that this time he doesn't say something wonderful but, instead, makes some "off color" remarks about Big Betty's dress. You, wanting him to feel as humiliated as Betty, make him stand in the corner with his thumb in his mouth and repeat "I'm an insensitive nincompoop." It is doubtful Billy will make fun of Betty again (and, truthfully, you wouldn't know about it if he did because you'd probably get fired for humiliating him). Punishment, however, does work.

However you choose to shape the Billy, it's important to remember that if you don't keep reinforcing the behavior in some way for an extended period, the behavior is bound to return to the way it was previously. I try to use positive first, negative second, and punishment as a last resort. If all this is too much work and takes too much time, just fire him and remove him as the unwanted stimulus. You are the scientist in this situation, go forth and box them in!

? **What's the BIG SECRET!?**

Your office cubicle is a Skinner Box. You can shape behavior if you're willing to be consistent in your own behavior.

The Secret To Being Likable (Not Liked)

If I had a voodoo doll, it would've been saturated with pins! There wasn't a day that he didn't frustrate me and, when I would confront him on his method, he'd say, "I'm not here to be your friend, Chip, I'm here to get a job done." I couldn't argue with that logic. And, even though he could be extremely difficult, I still found him likable.

Let's face it, leading isn't a popularity contest. It can't be. There will be decisions that we make and tasks we give as leaders that are going to be ill received, complained about, and tarried over. However unpopular, things need to get done. Too many leaders worry about being liked. This can become an immobilizing force that keeps us from moving forward. And, as my Chief told me, we aren't given the charge of leading to be friends....we're given that responsibility because things need to get done. My Chief understood this and didn't let the worry of being liked get in the way of mission. Yet, I found him likable and there wasn't much I wouldn't do when he asked. Here's why:

He was consistent. I always knew what to expect. His standards were high and I knew that if I brought him shoddy work, it would be returned. He didn't waive in his beliefs or how he wanted things done based on how the wind was blowing that day.

He communicated. Not only did I know what I needed to do and what the expectation was, I knew what he knew. He didn't keep secrets and would hear out my logic when I was trying to explain something.

He cared. I knew that he wanted me to succeed...that my success was, ultimately, his success. Further, he took the time to know about my family. If there was something on my mind, I could be sure it was on his mind too – both personal and professional.

He fostered cooperation. There was never any room for inter-departmental backstabbing and politics. Regardless of how we personally felt about each other, we had to work together if we were going to meet expectations.

Additionally, he wasn't too good to roll up his sleeves and work alongside us.

There's a lot to be said for being liked. In life, I like to be liked. However, I feel that there's a great divide between being liked and likable. Being liked as a leader is great as long as it doesn't get in the way of getting things done. So, don't get hung up on it. Not everything you do is going to be popular or well received. You're not always going to be liked! But, you can still be likable if you're consistent, communicate, care, and cooperate.

? **What's the BIG SECRET!?**
Worrying about being liked is the enemy of production.

The Secret To Talking About It Not Around It

As Marcellus Wallace said to Butch in Pulp Fiction, ***"We don't want to think, we want to know."***

Larry was a great guy to work for. He was, quite frankly, one of the nicest people I knew. So nice, in fact, that he would never talk directly about something that needed to be done (I think he hated giving tasks or feeling that he was giving orders). That, coupled with extensive vocabulary and his love of hearing himself talk, resulted in his talking around issues. He'd talk on top of it, underneath it, and on both sides, but never directly about it. I could never follow where he was or what needed to be done! Finally, exasperated, I said, "Look...I'm not smart enough to figure out what you are or aren't talking about. If you need something done, just tell me what it is." After that, he did.

Are you clear on your expectations to others or are you like Larry? People need clarity if the job is going to get done right or if it's going to get done at all. Want people to know? Here's how I've learned to do it.

Know what you want, exactly. I don't think this needs any further explanation.

Don't pontificate, use an economy of words. Save your huge vocabulary for the stories you tell. People's attention spans are short. The longer you talk, the less they listen. If you know what you want, exactly, say it.

Lastly, check for understanding and move on. Again, I don't think this needs further explanation.

Your team doesn't want to think they know, they want to know...EXACTLY! Further they won't know what you know or what you want until you let them know. Be clear and concise on what you want. Your team can't meet the expectation unless they know what the expectation is.

> ? **What's the BIG SECRET!?**
> People can't solve the problem if you aren't clear on what the problem is.

The Secret About Having The Conversation BEFORE You Have The Conversation

"Hey, I saw you walking up the street talking to someone...but no one was there" the Major said.

Yup, he was correct. You see, I have this really bad habit of going through potentially contentious conversations in my head prior to having them. The bad part is that I get so into the conversation that my lips move and I (usually) use hand gestures. On this particular day, I was talking (in my head) to the comptroller on justifying my budget.

Yes, this can make me look a little crazy...walking around, talking to people that aren't there (no sound comes out, just my lips move). However, going through every possible scenario before a difficult conversation helps me keep my cool and not make a scene. Further, it's helped me map out the logical sequencing of events, not leave anything on the table and have that "Man, I should've said this!" moment after.

How about you? Ever get caught off guard and felt unprepared during a difficult conversation? If so, try having it ahead of time. When I have it ahead of time, I go through these possibilities.

I think about worst case scenario. What's the worst way the conversation can go? What will I say? What are my major points and how will I respond when things start going bad? How am I going to keep my cool and not make things worse? (I don't have anger issues, but I do have triggers.)

I also think about best case scenario. If the stars align and manna starts falling from heaven, how will I respond? What words will I use to express my appreciation? How do I lead the conversation to best case (i.e. showing the value of my side).

Last, I think about how I am going to close. Best case or worst case, I want to make sure I leave the conversation on an upbeat note. I also want to make sure I don't forget anything so I'll make a mental note of the follow up things that need to be done.

These are methods I use for being prepared for potentially combative conversations before having them. Using this method has helped me stay in control of my emotions when my emotions want to control me and keep things on point. I hope they help you too. If you do try using these steps, just try to keep your lips from moving when you have the conversation in your head or, as I've started doing, wear your bluetooth earpiece so it looks like you're talking to someone on the phone (you'll look less crazy when you're walking up the street).

> ? **What's the BIG SECRET!?**
> Practicing conversations ahead of time doesn't make it perfect, it just makes you prepared.

The Secret To (Gracefully) Walking Away From a Time Parasite

Damon couldn't believe that I just left in the middle of the conversation and left him hanging. Later on, he came to my office and I explained the art of walking away.

Although Damon and I were both Lieutenants (and contemporaries), I had a lot more time in the Navy than he did and had learned, the hard way, that there are a lot of people in the workplace who don't value your time. They are nice enough people but, if they corner you, they can yammer on about a lot of things that just don't matter. Our Chief Staff Officer was one of those people. I don't know if he was lonely (or hug deprived) but if he caught you in the passage way he'd undoubtedly tell you the same story he had told you 10 times before and, before you knew it, he'd wasted nearly 30 minutes of your time on things that were nice, but didn't pertain to anything that needed to be done.

Don't get me wrong...I am not against being social at work. I think sharing stories are one of the best ways of connecting with people and reinforcing organizational norms. However, the conversations with the Chief Staff Officer did nothing but put me behind on my work (and I had too much to do). On that day, he stopped Damon and I, began to roll into one of his pointless sea stories and I held up a piece of paper and left.

Do you work with any time parasites? If so, here are a few strategies I shared with Damon on how to walk away with grace.

No matter where you're going at work, carry a piece of paper with you. Truthfully, it doesn't even need to be an important piece of paper. Only you know what's on there. If you're cornered, hold it up and say, "gotta take care of this" and walk away.

Another strategy is to look pissed off. I've been blessed with a naturally furrowed brow. I'm happy and friendly enough but my "thinking face" is one of disdain. This is a natural repellant to those who wish to waste your time. If you want a conversation, smile. If not, don't. (You can even mumble to yourself for effect if you wish.)

Lastly, give them the "be right back" and then don't come back. Say it with a smile and with eye contact (it has to be believable). Later, if questioned on why you didn't come back, tell the truth that you got overwhelmed with work (which is normally true in today's workplace).

Again, if you have the time for being social and sharing stories, do it. Sharing stories are the cornerstone of an effective organization. However, beware of the time parasites. If you get cornered and don't have time, then just walk away.

?

What's the BIG SECRET!?
No one cares about your time like you.
It's okay to walk away.

The Secret About Having a Donut Policy

WHAT!? Why didn't I know this? My door is always open!

Recently, I heard from a former student and he relayed to me how, in a staff meeting, his new boss let the staff know he had an open door policy. The boss then explained the parameters of the policy, "I have an open door policy. Just make sure you clear it through your supervisor first and set up an appointment. I don't want anyone to just 'pop' in whenever they feel like it." My former student then stated, "I think my boss is a little confused on what an open door policy is." Unfortunately, an open door (or a policy to go with it) isn't enough to keep up on what is going on around you (and this type of policy certainly doesn't encourage an open exchange).

I personally think that if you have to state you have an "open door policy" you don't have one. What this manager really needs is not an "open door policy" but a "donut policy." What's a donut policy? It's where you bring in a dozen once a week, throw them on the table in the break room, and hang out for a while. ***Let's face it, donuts:***

- **Have a magnetic force that draw people from their cubicles.**
- **Encourage people to engage in conversation while eating them.**
- **Make the coffee taste better.**

If you have a Donut policy, you don't need an open door policy. With a donut policy, you learn about what's going on, get to know your people and, through the power of tastiness, they'll know you're accessible enough to walk through your door when a problem arises. Don't wait! Pick up a dozen of "nature's perfect food" and connect today!

?

What's the BIG SECRET!?
Bridges built with people that are constructed with donuts are sweet to travel.

The Secret About Competition!

The stench of apathy permeated our department. I had been there for about a month and had watched as my team floundered on figuring out what needed to be done and how they were going to get it done. We had metrics that we were judged by, but admittedly, there was a whole pointlessness to doing them (as they were always in flux) and no reward for doing them well. This pointlessness permeated my team and they slipped into an apathetic, Who cares what happens?" kind of mentality. They needed a jolt!

There are many things that motivate, but, for teams, I think competition works best. I don't think I'm alone in not liking others who are more successful than me. (Not personally, but professionally.) I don't think that makes me a bad person, it just makes me human. It's at the heart of competition. We like to win! We like to have bragging rights.

Further, everyone likes to be on a winning team! With this in mind, I manufactured a competition to get this team moving.

MANUFACTURED!? Yes! I manufactured it. Some competitions are easy to see and others have to be made up. It may seem a bit manipulative, but, like I said, this team needed a jump start (okay, I said jolt) and, once in motion, teams tend to stay in motion. How do you manufacture a competition?

First, pick a benchmark. For this venture, I picked the command whose metrics were consistently better than ours. They had no idea I had targeted them and, most likely, didn't care but they gave us the fuel for the competition.

Second, plan to kick butt. I went to my team and talked to them about our competition and asked how we could drive this other command into the ground. They came up with great ideas on how to boost our metrics. I also asked them on what would be the reward for when we did it. Again, they came up with some good ideas *(NOTE: I had to shoot down "a circus clown keg party" (they were a creative crew))*.

Third, kick butt. With marching orders in hand, we stepped out and executed the plan. We talked about where we were and where we were going every day. Further, if one team member started slacking, another would do some "peer to peer" coaching to get that person moving again. ***As momentum built so did the excitement on reaching the goal.***

Lastly, bring in the clowns. Even though I shot down the circus clown keg party, when we "SMOKED" the other command we did celebrate. Celebrate as big or small as the goal dictates. I don't think you can go too big (as long as no one ends up getting hurt or in jail).

What's funny is that the metrics we picked ended up being the ones that my boss was being judged by and not only did we get bragging rights but he did too. Perhaps I should have asked him about priorities before I manufactured the competition but, in the end, it worked out.

> **?** **What's the BIG SECRET!?**
> Everyone likes to be on a winning team. Success brings more success!

The Secret About Finesse

This may be hard to believe but I have been accused of being somewhat abrupt. I have filters but I, mostly, let people know what I think. It goes with my life philosophy of trying to live a life free of hypocrisy. I'm not alone. My four brothers have the same problem. It's in our genes. Gene's genes to be exact (from our Father, Eugene). My brother, Matt (also a Navy Veteran and my best friend), has had to grapple with his mouth overriding his brain too. One such time came shortly after September 11th, 2001.

After the terrorists attacked the Pentagon, Matt, came to work at the Washington Navy Yard (where I was serving as the Director of Security) to be the liaison between the military and the families of those who died on that tragic day. It was a stressful job. He worked long days and dealt with not only the bureaucracy within the military but also with delicate matters of the heart - tending to those who had lost a loved one. One day, a cocky administration officer came down to his office and informed Matt that he was taking one of his copiers. When he asked which one he could take, Matt pointed to one and said, "that one." The officer asked, "Why that one?" To which Matt replied, "Because that one's broken and I don't need it." Infuriated, the officer said a few choice words and stormed out of the office. Granted, this may not seem like a big deal but, within the rank structure of the military (Matt being junior to this officer), it ruffled this officer's feathers enough that he couldn't stop talking about "that insubordinate Chief downstairs" for weeks.

Over 10 years later we still laugh about that situation and he'll still state, "What else was I supposed to say? I couldn't let him have the working copier, I needed it to get the job done!" He says that in jest because, over the years, we've both learned how to "package" what we say so that it doesn't explode in others' faces and we can still stay true to who we are. How do we package?

First, try to understand. I try to start with asking questions. With the case of the broken copier, asking the questions of why, what for and how long would've have opened a dialogue and (at least) made that particular officer feel heard. The workplace is full of scrimmages for power. Going on the offensive causes others to do the same and, pretty soon, all we have are emotional people talking and not listening. Asking question and listening sets a tone of understanding and then allows you to be heard.

Second, state your case. (Okay, state your case in a non-explosive way.) In this case, I don't know if Matt had stated his case it would have made any difference (this officer was not a good listener). However, I like to believe that it would have. My experience has been that reasonable people can reach reasonable solutions when logic is present and when stated free of emotion. That's how to package! After I state my case, if I I want to put a bow on the package, I'll be empathetic with the cause and share a smile (if appropriate).

To this day, all of us five boys grapple with Gene's genes and our mouth's want to override our brain. Seeking to understand first by asking questions and then stating our case has helped me (and my brother) package things in such a way that they doesn't explode in another's face. I hope it helps you do the same!

> ?
>
> **What's the BIG SECRET!?**
> How you say it and how you present it matters. When in doubt, smile.

The Secret About Meeting Proxies

The only thing I dislike more than other people's drama is other people's meetings. Let's face it, most meetings are dull, uneventful, and full of narcoleptic inducing briefings. I like my meetings fun, quick, and to the point. If you're finding yourself going to more meetings in the dull category, might I suggest getting a "meeting proxy?"

During my last tour in Washington, DC, I was "invited" to many meetings. I had more meetings than one person could possibly want (or handle) on their own. Some days, I would have back to back meetings for 8 hours! After about six months of trying to attend every meeting I could, I had finally hit my breaking point. After careful thought, I brought one of my trusted division heads in and informed him, from that point forward would attend meetings in my stead. He would attend, pay attention, and then let me know if I had to go to the next one (some meetings were meetings to talk about the next meeting). If I didn't need to be at the next one, he was in charge of the meeting in perpetuity. He would have the full authority to act on my behalf at that meeting. He, on that day, became my proxy at all meetings!

Having someone to go to meetings for me freed up time for me to deal with personnel issues and the personal issues my people had. They needed a leader that was present, not one who was presently in a meeting. It also made my division head feel valued. Although we kidded about the title, he felt good that he was trusted to speak on our department's behalf on important matters. Further, he knew I always had his back if something went awry. You can delegate authority but not responsibility. Regardless of how many meetings he went to, the responsibility always laid with me.

If you're not high enough in the chain to select a meeting proxy, I'd suggest asking if you could be one. I spent many years going to meetings for my bosses. It gave me a holistic knowledge of how things worked. I think that knowledge made me a better team member and helped lead to faster promotions.

Whether you're on the selection end or on the receiving end, there's not a bad side to having a meeting proxy (or being one). The key to success in this endeavor is to keep open lines of communication and trust at all times. When either is breached, it's over.

Give yourself some time or gain yourself an education and proxy it up today!

> ? **What's the BIG SECRET!?**
> You can do more and learn more if you let go and trust your team to act in your stead.

The Secret About Classifying Problems

"DAD! He's looking at me!" "DAD! She's in my space!" "DAD! He ate the last cookie!" Okay, the last one was me. I ate the last cookie. I learned early on, as a parent, that I couldn't insert myself into every tiff that my kids had. Nor could I shelter them from the outside world. If I did, I wasn't really preparing them for real life and how to work things out with others or work in their environment. Quite frankly, there were many things that I just didn't care about.

I think there are many parallels between parenting and leading people. Some might disagree but, in the end, I will call **"SHENANIGANS!"** on their argument and continue to believe what I believe. One such parallel is that of inserting ourselves into everything that goes on between our people and in their environment. When we insert ourselves in matters they can handle, we aren't doing them any favors. People need to know how to figure things out. To help myself in this, I classify most things one of two ways:

1. ***Things I care about***
2. ***Things I don't care about***

Generally, the things I care about are the things that immediately impact me and my ability to get the job done. This may seem a bit narcissistic and Chip-centric, but it's not. I group into this category the health and welfare of my team; things and/or people that degrade morale; getting the job done; and creating an atmosphere where people feel valued. There are a lot more things I care about but these are a few.

In the category of things I don't care about are excuses; what kind of car you drive; and that there's no good food in the vending machine. Most of all, what I don't care about is OPD (Other People's Drama). (Kind of like with my kids.) With an ex-wife and teenagers, I have enough drama of my own. I don't want to get sucked into the gaping black hole of who is doing what to whom and how I should get involved. Most drama has an expiration date and, if I involve myself, I've expended time and energy that could have been used elsewhere. Further, I've kept another from learning how to work it out.

All that being said, I am not against listening. As a leader, I am always open to listening. I will listen but will also save my energy where it is best suited. If it's something that you can work out, you will be fully empowered to go forth, do good deeds and work it out.

Back fill me on how it went. Like I said, I'm happy to listen. If it is something that I need to be involved with, I will be.

In the end, there are only so many hours in a day and so much energy that can be expended. Diluting yourself with things you don't care about gives poor results and doesn't empower others to make a difference for themselves. Figure out what you do and don't care about and respond accordingly.

> ?
>
> **What's the BIG SECRET!?**
> Focus your time and attention on things you really care about and empower others to do the same.

The Secret About What To Do After You Classify A Problem

He called an emergency meeting of the Department Heads. We sat there, looking at each other, wondering why the Captain had called the meeting. As he came in, we all stood until told to take our seats. As we sat we could see the worry on his face. He looked down at his pad of paper, then up at us and said, "Gentlemen, gasoline is going up over $3 a gallon. We're going to need to do something so that people can afford to come to work." We all looked at each other confused. Granted, we all pay more now and are used to it but, for him (at this time), this was a real crisis.

I immediately thought back to the best piece of advice I've ever gotten on solving problems from my friend, Steve. When facing a personal crisis he told me, "Chip, all problems can be classified one of two ways: They are either solvable or unsolvable." He went on to add that even when unsolvable, they might still be workable. I have taken this advice into every leadership job I've had. Classifying them this way has saved me time, worry and effort. Here's how the classification works.

Solvable. The problem has an answer that you and the team can develop. You, personally, may not know the solution but, with a strong "why," the team will find a way. This is a problem that is within your control. Know the difference.

Unsolvable. The problem has no solution. If it has no solution, why waste your time "trying to rearrange deck chairs on the Titanic?" Unsolvable problems usually consist of things that are completely out of your control but you may still worry about. If you can't control it, why worry and stress? Classify it as unsolvable and move on.

Unsolvable but workable. This problem is out of your control but there may be actions you and the team can alleviate some of the ill effects of the problem. Such was the case with gas prices.

Although it was unsolicited, I shared this classification with the other Department Heads. We then classified this problem as "Unsolvable but workable." We came up with some solutions to alleviate the ill effects of gas prices rising and put the Captain at ease.

We all face problems. If you're anything like me, you worry about things. Some things you can control and some you can't. Try classifying them as solvable or unsolvable. Bring your team together and brainstorm possibilities. If it's solvable or workable, take action. If it's unsolvable and not workable, let it go. Either way, you'll gain peace of mind, less stress, and come out on top.

> ? **What's the BIG SECRET!?**
> Focus on what you can control or what is uncontrollable will control you.

The Secret About Asking For Help

RIP!!! The seam in the back of my dress uniform pants completely gave out. Admittedly, I had packed on some serious pounds. I had quit smoking and substituted the smokes for anything sweet around. (Okay, that's just an excuse...I love donuts and had had a continual stream of them going into my mouth.)

That morning was our Winter Uniform Inspection. As Commanding Officer, I was the inspecting officer of our 300 reserve personnel. I didn't know what I was going to do since that was my only pair of inspection pants so I called my brother (who was also in the Navy and lived a couple of miles away) to see if I could borrow his pants. After listening to his stream of laughter and ribbing, he said, "Chip, I'm not home and, besides, I'm two inches shorter than you and you'd look like a buffoon wearing highwaters!"

On my drive to work I went through the possibilities. One option was to cancel the inspection. Another was to delegate the inspecting officer position to another officer. Both of those were great at "saving face" but not in keeping with the way I like to lead from the front.

When I got to work, I quickly scurried to my office and sat in my chair. I had an hour until the inspection and a decision needed to be made. I needed help. In desperation, I called my staff into the office. Being summoned at 0630 was uncommon and I could see their concern as they entered my office. When they were all present I stood up, turned around, starting laughing and said, "I need some help!" The entire office erupted in laughter. After it subsided, it was a mad dash to find me a pair of pants. The entire team searched every locker in the place and (with 20 minutes left to inspection) they found me a pair.

This "event" was embarrassing but I wouldn't have been able to do what I needed to do without the help of my team. If I had held on to my ego and gone with the options of copping out of the inspection, I would have not been fulfilling my obligations as a leader. Further, I wouldn't have felt good about myself after. By letting go of my ego, laughing about the mistake and eliciting help from the team, I was able to fulfill my obligations.

We all have things that happen that we're embarrassed about. It's easy to sit back, fret, and try to save face. In the end, we're all human. Mistakes are part of living. Why fret!? Why not laugh it off and reach out for help? **When we, as leaders, can laugh at our own mistakes it gives others permission to do the same and creates an atmosphere where people can take risks without fear of reprise.**

I did the inspection and, after, put on a uniform that fit a bit better. That entire weekend's duty with my team was light, productive and it all started when we laughed at me showing my ass.

> ?
> **What's the BIG SECRET!?**
> Show some skin and don't be afraid to ask for help.

The Secret About How To Degrade Trust

I sat there, diligently typing, as Kimmie rolled her chair over to mine when Georgette left the office. I knew what was coming. It happened every day. One person would leave the office and the other would roll over and say, "Do you know what she did!?" They would then proceed to unload their grievances about the other person. Then, when that person would come back and the other leave, it would happen again with the person that was just complained about to me complaining about the other person. It wasn't always the same people complaining about the others. It rotated. These two about one. One about the other two. One about just one. Hey, at least it was varied.

Finally, one day, Kimmie said to me, "You know what I like about you, Chip? You don't talk about other people!" WHAT?! I knew better than to engage. If I engaged, then I would be the one in the middle. What I learned was that, regardless of circumstance, it's never a bad policy to just keep it to yourself.

Granted, many of the people irritated me. Sometimes, they'd irritate me to the point that I wanted to scream...but I just kept it to myself. I didn't sit in quiet desperation, I talked to TRUSTED people outside the workspace about how best to deal with a situation, but I would not engage in idle gossip.

Let's face it...we, as humans, LOVE THE GOSSIP! Don't engage, keep it to yourself. Better yet, remember what your mom told you about not saying anything if you don't have something nice to say.

You'll gain more respect and people will know that they can trust you and then you'll know everything!

?

What's the BIG SECRET!?
If you're talking about others with others then they know you'll talk about them too.

The Secret About Strategic Change

Have you ever felt like there is so much to do that you don't know what to do and it immobilizes you? I know it's happened to me more than once. In the case of my role as Director of Security, we went from "rags to riches" within a year because I took the focus off the "me" and put it on the "we." Despair is never the answer but collective action is. Are you trying to get it all done? Don't know where to start? Are you overwhelmed? Do you want to crawl back in bed and throw the blankets over your head? I've been there, done that, and have the pillow marks on my face to prove it. Here is what's worked for me in moving the team forward; I know it can work for you too.

First, look to your team. Your teammates are the ones doing the job. They've been in the trenches. They know what to do. In the case of my job as Director of Security, I pulled all of my supervisors in and asked them where I should start. WE then prioritized the list and stepped out in action on getting things done. I, personally, like to start with the easy things first. It helps with a sense of accomplishment and building momentum. (I also like things on my "ta done" list and not my "ta do" list). As a leader, it's impossible to know everything, but you have to trust that your team does. Get the people who know together.

Second, before you make a change, give it the sniff test. Any guy knows what the sniff test is. For those who don't...if the laundry doesn't smell dirty, you can get another day of wear out of it without washing it. On our list, there were MANY suggestions of what people wanted now. But, truthfully, there's a great divide between WANT and NEED. For instance, I may WANT a new Corvette, but I need basic transportation. For our team, I just asked before making a change that we give it a sniff test. Could we get "another day" out of what was going on and focus in on what NEEDED to go in the laundry that day. That simple test saved us time, effort, and resources. It also helped us stay laser focused on needs and not wants. So, before making a change...just give it sniff.

Third, I like to see what works and do more of that. From that "list day" forward, we'd meet every week to talk about what was going on, how things were progressing and what worked. If something was working, I'd say "lets do more of that." If it didn't work, we'd take a look at why and then decide to "not do any more of that." Some ideas sound great in concept but don't always pan out the way we want. Those are the ones we don't want to do (even though we might be emotionally invested in them). Let it go and do more of what works.

These aren't the only things we did. We also created a vision, policies, and procedures for things as we moved forward. **But we first had to actually start moving forward**. In today's world of doing more with less (and less), it's easy to get stuck at the cross roads of despair and action - wondering what to do when there's so much to do. In those instances, pull the covers down off your face, put your feet on the floor and step out with your team.

> ? **What's the BIG SECRET!?**
> Spend your time working on the things that need work.

The Secret About Giving People Choices

With our business being complete and coffee remaining in our cups, our conversation turned to children. With each of us having multiple children, Eliz and I always have many stories to share and, immediately, I went to one of (what I consider) a premier parenting moment. **Begin story flashback....**

It was 2002 and we lived right outside of Washington, DC. I had (as usual) gotten to work early that day and had just gotten back to my office when my phone rang.

"She did what!?" I said incredulously. I couldn't believe it. My darling baby girl had gotten in trouble at school for spitting on another student. Now, it wasn't the first time she had gotten in trouble at school (nor would it be the last), but I was still amazed she would do THAT! I said that I would handle it when I got home and went back to work while mulling over the course of action for her punishment.

When I walked in the house, there she sat, head down, and sheepishly looking up at me (as though her sad face was going to make a difference).

I said, "I hear you had a bit of trouble at school today....what's the deal?"

She then explained that there was this boy that was always teasing her and that, today, she just got tired of it and spit on him. Then, of course, I explained that wasn't the way it should have been handled, explained how it should be handled and then asked her what she thought her punishment should be. "I don't know," Victoria replied.

"Well," I said, "I've been mulling it over a bit and I have two options for you."

Victoria's head perked up when she heard she had options.

I continued, "You can either write this sentence about how we don't spit 500 times OR you can take this 3 pound coffee can and fill it with spit."

"I'll take that one!" she said enthusiastically about the coffee can.

"Okay," I said, "but you have to sit here in the kitchen until it's full." and I left her to her do her duty.

Not even five minutes later a raspy voice fainted out a cry

from the kitchen, "DAD....DAD....DAD..." and I returned to see how she was coming along. She (after just a few minutes) had run out of spit. "Dad, " Victoria whispered, "can I do the sentences instead?" I obliged and she has never spit on anyone again.

End story flashback.

When I finished telling the story, Eliz and I laughed, I sat there (still basking triumphantly after 10 years) enjoying my proud parenting moment.

Eliz then said, "It's all about choices...giving people (and children) choices YOU can live with as leader."

I sat and thought. I had never really thought about it like that before from a leadership position. There were many times I had not offered choices and then when the person was given a a self generated choice, I couldn't oblige with the request. Conversely, when I had offered choices to others in a tenuous situation that I could live with, we nearly always both came out winners.

Here are two reasons it works.

First, giving people a choice you can live with puts the control in their hands. Granted, it's not ALL in their hands but that piece is. We ALL want to have control of our destinies. It helps us shine, flourish, and be treated as humans.

Second, it gets rid of the pony. If I had asked Victoria what she wanted as a punishment, anything could have happened. Much like when you ask what a kid wants at Christmas....they want a PONY! I don't have a pony to give. In today's business world, we only have so much to give. If someone asks for a pony and you can't give it, they feel cheated and you may feel bad for not being able to give them what is wanted (or maybe not). Get rid of the option of the pony.

How to you make it work? Ask yourself these three questions:

What does the person want?
What two things are doable?
Can I live with either choice?

Granted, I knew Victoria couldn't fill a coffee can with spit but that was a completely different scenario than what we face most days at work. Eliz was right, can can't do everything but we can do some things - giving people a choice is one of those things. Step up, take charge, and give people a choice.

> ?
> **What's the BIG SECRET!?**
> Giving people choices you, as leader, can live with is a win/win!

The Secret About Perception

WHY did I climb it!? It could have been because it was there. It might have been because I was feeling "youthful" after spending the day with family and friends. There could have just been a brief interruption of oxygen to my brain that impaired my decision making ability. Regardless of the reason, I found myself 12 feet off the ground, sitting on a branch in a tree, pondering how I was going to get down. Noticing my conundrum, my wife, Gwen, rushed up to the tree to offer assistance. Not wanting to be a bother, I let her know that I could get down on my own.

"No, I'll go get a ladder," she insisted.

I maintained that I was quite capable of getting out of this on my own and, as she stepped away, I leaped from the branch to the ground. OUCH!! I landed hard! All 220 pounds of me belly flopped onto the earth below.

As I laid there, face down (with a small puff of dust emerging with every exhale), Gwen asked sheepishly, "Are you okay?"

"Yes, I'm fine," I replied. "I thought I was much closer to the ground."

"Hmm, perception isn't always reality, is it!?" she said.

Truer words could have not been spoken. My perception was that I WAS much closer to the ground. The reality was, I wasn't. My perception was the I WAS very "cat like" and agile. The reality was, I wasn't. My perception was that I WAS as light as I was when I was 10 and regularly jumped from trees. The reality was that I've eaten WAY too many donuts to even think that was true. As I hobbled to the house to grab some ibuprofen and an ice pack, I thought about those words: "***perception not being reality***." How true that had been in SO many situations I had faced in my life. Delving into a situation without looking at the reality almost always resulted in a bad outcome - losing time, money, or even (as in this case) causing pain.

Not to negate the power of possibility, but if you'd like to move ahead faster, smarter, and with less pain, here's how to do it realistically:

1. **Rely on pictures, not mirrors.** Let's face it, mirrors lie to us. When I look in a mirror, I see exactly what I want to see. When I see a picture, I see what is really there. To get the reality of a situation, we need to get a good picture of what it is from other people. Ask questions of those who you know are familiar or can give you an accurate assessment of a situation. Relying on your own perception of the situation without getting a clear picture from others is not reality and can trip the evolution up.

2. **Manage the reality.** When I manage the perception of a situation and not the reality, I can spend an inordinate amount of time working on (and worrying about) things that don't matter and don't contribute in getting the result I need. Conversely, if I work on what is REAL, I can allocate the right resources, time, and energy to what needs to get done. In today's world of limited resources (including my own time), I need to concentrate everything I have strategically to what is real.

3. **Accept (and even ask for) help.** There are two schools of thought when looking at bringing others in on solving a situation or reaching a goal. One is, "too many cooks spoil the broth." The other is, "many hands make light work." If you have gotten a clear picture of what the situation is and you

are managing the reality of what is going on, you will know which philosophy will apply to this situation. If I had accepted (or even asked) for help in getting out of that tree, I would have had a MUCH better result.

After a month of hobbling around and eating ibuprofen like gummi bears, I finally healed and am "wiser for the wear." Could I have jumped out of that tree like a 10 year old "cat like" boy without injury to my body (or pride)? Sure, it was possible...but not probable. Please be aware, I am NEVER against possibility. Possibility takes us places we never thought we could go. However, I could have avoided all of that down time and pain if I had gotten a clear picture, managed the reality, and accepted help (and realized that my perception of the situation was NOT the reality).   When we add reality to possibility we not only perceive things clearer, we also increase the PROBABILITY of getting done what we need to get done.

?

What's the BIG SECRET!?
Perception is NOT reality! Don't assume, dig a little deeper.

The Secret About Language Barriers

It was January, 2009, and (of course) I had come down with my usual Winter sinus infection. And this one was not your "run of the mill" infection. It was the kind that made me thirsty all of the time - so much, in fact, that my throat would get so dry that I felt that I could barely speak. Also, as luck would have it, this wonderful condition struck me the day before I was to leave on a trip to Costa Rica. Prior to my trip, I tried everything to shake it....water, orange juice, airborne, and several "home cooked" remedies I found via google and nothing worked.

With no change in my condition on the day of my trip, I headed down to O'Hare airport to start the journey. The dryness in the back of my throat and the pounding in my forehead didn't detour me from keeping a smile on my face as I shimmied through security and onto my plane. The trip was long and I was miserable. No matter how much water I drank, my throat was still on fire.

During our exchange through Guatemala (where we had to de-plane and re-board while men with machine guns stood close by), I felt a little out of place trying to figure out what they were saying relying solely on what Spanish I had picked up listening to Ricky Martin songs but persevered. When I got back on the plane, I fell dead asleep until we landed in San Jose. Having been asleep and with no fluids, I could barely utter a word my throat was so dry when I awoke...I had to get something to drink! I rushed off the airplane and started looking for the closest place to get a beverage and then, in the distance, I saw the Golden Arches! Hooray!! I rushed up, got in line and started gleaning the menu for something recognizable. After what seemed like hours, it was my turn. I looked the server behind the counter and said, "Orange drink, please"

"Que?" he responded.

I replied louder, "Orange Drink, Please!"

Looking me directly back he said, "Que!?"

Exasperated, I mustered the loudest voice I could and yelled, "ORANGE DRINK!"

Just then, a fellow passenger from my flight tapped my on

the shoulder and said, "You can yell as loud as you want, sir, he won't understand you if you're not speaking the language." Try this, " Soda de Naranja, por favor!"

The server immediately understood, got me my drink and I was able to douse the flame in the back of my throat. As I was walking away, I starting thinking about what my fellow passenger had said. "He won't understand if you're not speaking the language."

How true that had been in so many aspects my life. Many times as a leader I had spoken louder and louder but my team hadn't understood what I was saying because I hadn't been speaking their language.

Has the same been true for you? How many times have you tried to get your message understood but, because you weren't speaking the language, you couldn't get through? If you want to go native, speak the language, and be understood, here are three things that you need to do.

Get a Tutor

Navigating the trails of a foreign land can be difficult if you don't have a guide. The same is true for learning the language of the people around you. Find someone that is fluent in both languages to help you translate what you want to say to how you need to say it. You won't be disappointed in having a translator.

Immerse Yourself In the Culture

Learning the language of your team can't be done if you're living in a different country (also known as your office or cubicle). Get out and about and learn what is important to them, what they do, and how they do it.

Practice

Practice makes perfect. In your journey, will you make some mistakes? Sure you will, however, the effort you make in trying to speak the native language will be admired and respected by the people around you. You might even find that they'll help you translate themselves and forgive a misstep due to your effort in appreciating who they are as people.

As leaders, it's our responsibility to make the steps necessary to not only be understood, but to first make the steps to understand our team. Speaking their language helps us do just that. I hope you try these three strategies for going native. I think you'll find that you'll no longer have to speak loud, you'll just have to speak up.

> ? **What's the BIG SECRET!?**
> You can yell as loud as you want...they won't understand you unless you're speaking the same language.

The Secret About Working With A Jackass

My work life has been peppered with people that have been...well let's just say, jackasses. I've always thought of myself as someone that's easy to get along with, but obviously, that's not the case with everyone. It could be your boss, co-worker, subordinate, or even the barista at Starbucks...let's face facts, we all work with some people that we might consider difficult. The difficulty could arise from a difference of opinion, attitude, or from breathing the same air. Regardless of the origin, it can make our work life miserable! If our work life is miserable, that's going to filter into most facets of the rest of our life. 80% of our success in life isn't about how much we know or how skilled we are; success comes from how well we get along with people and those difficult ones can be, well, difficult!

If you'd like to get along with (notice I wrote "get along with" and not be "best friends with") the difficult people at work, here are three tactics that have always worked for me.

Tactic #1: KEEP IT PROFESSIONAL!

When I was a young Petty Officer, I worked with a crusty old Master Chief that, quite frankly, hated my guts (and it was reciprocated). I didn't like the way he did things and he didn't like my "snarky" attitude. So, to get along and get things done, we kept it professional. Very much like Dragnet's, Joe Friday, our conversations were about "just the facts." That kept personality out of the equation and kept things moving.

Tactic #2: BE NICE

My first instinct when someone comes at me is to come right back. If they bring a knife to a fight, I want to bring a gun (figuratively...obviously). Although it goes against my instinct, what I've found is that by being nice, it helps ease the tension. If they bring a knife, I'm bringing a smile. If they bring a gun, I'm bringing a laugh (you get the idea). Take a clue from Patrick Swayze in "Road House"...."Be nice, until it's time not to be nice." Those times may come, but 99.9% of the time we can be nice, kill them with kindness and always come out ahead.

Tactic #3: FIND SOMETHING IN COMMON

I used to have a Major work for me that would try and block anything (and everything) he could in order to maintain control. Instinctively (like I said), I flanked the same way but found that fighting fire with fire brought less results than I would hope. What I found was that if I started any conversation about daughters (we both had two), he would be much more receptive to anything I had to say. I would even ask his advice on what he did in certain situations when he was raising his girls (his were a little older than mine). EVERYONE HAS SOMETHING IN COMMON! Find out what it is by asking questions and let that be the baseline for opening your conversations. Even if it's "Hey, you have parents!? I have parents too!" We ALL have a baseline from which to draw and connect.

In all of these situations, I didn't become BFF's with the person but I DID learn to get along. In any situation, we have a choice to make. We can let it control us or we can work to control it.

> ?
>
> **What's the BIG SECRET!?**
> Everyone has something in common.
> Break it down to the core and connect.

The Secret About Listening Better

Yes, I'll admit it...I'm a terrible listener. I have the best of intentions of hanging on every word that is said, but usually, I drift. But, it's not my fault! I have these crazy monkeys jumping around in my head at all times! One monkey causes me to babble, another one causes distractions and the host of others just jump around throwing things at each other! Okay, there are no monkeys...but sometimes it feels like there are! However, knowing that I am a poor listener is the first step in my becoming a better listener.

In today's world, I don't think I'm alone. I would venture to say that we all struggle at one point or another with our ability to listen. Listening is a distinct asset and a skill that can be continually honed. Do you struggle with monkeys? Do they keep you from listening too? If so, try these 4 strategies that will help you listen better!

***LISTENING STRATEGY NUMBER ONE*: SHUT UP!**

REALLY!? The first step in being a better listener is to shut up? YOU BETCHA!! There's no way you can hear another person if you're yammering about something or thinking about yammering about something. If you want to say something....DON'T! If you are thinking about saying something...DON'T! ZIP IT and concentrate on the person that is speaking. Your turn to speak will come soon enough.

LISTENING STRATEGY NUMBER TWO: **PAY ATTENTION**

What is being said is not nearly as important as how it is being said. If you aren't paying attention, you'll miss 80% of the content! Listen for feelings, voice inflection, and watch body language. I can't tell you how many things I misinterpreted when I wasn't fully paying attention. I've ended up at the wrong place at the wrong time and in the wrong attire (and that's a benign example). Don't wander, make and keep eye contact when possible and stay in the moment.

***LISTENING STRATEGY NUMBER THREE:* KILL THE MONKEY**

Monkeys in my brain cause distractions. You want to kill the monkey? Get rid of the distractions! He'll die of boredom and won't cause you any more grief. The biggest distraction for me my computer! Quite frankly, my children capitalize on this and will purposely ask me for expensive trappings while I am on it. I agreed to spend a fortune on items that I remember nothing about because the monkey hadn't been properly euthanized. You know what YOUR monkeys are...kill THEM!!

LISTENING STRATEGY NUMBER FOUR: **REPEAT IT**

You've accomplished the first three strategies and think you know what's been said...now repeat it back to the person that was speaking. You don't have to do it verbatim (actually, I'd paraphrase it...repeating back verbatim is a little bit creepy). If you've gotten something wrong, they'll let you know. If not, you've tried your best to get the gist of the conversation and/or issue down to the best of your ability. BRAVO!

Like I said, I struggle with listening all of the time. I can blame it on monkeys, computers, children, or the fact that I grew up as part of the Sesame Street generation and I'm used to everything being spoon fed to me at an elementary level. Whatever the cause, I can continue to work on listening better every day (and so can you).

> ?
>
> **What's the BIG SECRET!?**
> Listening is a skill that can always improve. Being present is a present to your team.

The Secret About Performance Appraisals

Giving someone their annual performance appraisal can be tricky if you aren't mentally prepared. My first crack at debriefing someone was an eye opening experience! I had plenty of years on the opposite side of the desk (getting told how I was performing) and thought I knew how I wanted it to go but found myself ill-prepared when it came down to executing it properly. I quickly got a system down and, after hundreds of practice runs, here's what you need to know:

1. **Perception is NOT reality!** People's perceptions of what they do and how they do are much different from yours. A good way to check this is to simply ask, "how do you feel things are going for you here, Bob?" (I just used Bob because we all know a Bob). Doing this allows you to assess where

they "think" they are versus where they might actually be. If they are the same.....FANTASTIC! If not, chances are you've done a poor job of communicating how they're doing through the year.

2. **Be Prepared!** I absolutely HATED when my bosses would ask me for my input on my annual evaluation, but really wanted me to write it for them. On one hand, it was great to toot my own horn, but on the other, it was somewhat disheartening to think that the person I had pledged my loyalty to for a year couldn't take an hour to recap all of my great accomplishments. Keep a log book or accomplishments folder on each team member to record noteworthy things and not so noteworthy things. Let them know about the folder so that they can contribute to it if they'd like to (also let them see it when asked so you don't have to visit HR unnecessarily). Prior to your debrief meeting, go through EVERYTHING to make sure you haven't missed anything so you won't have to rely on memory.

3. **Be Personable!** Make people comfortable! Getting debriefed on your performance can be some stressful stuff. I always knew I worked hard but always wondered how things were going to go on the evaluation debrief. Pick a quiet spot, welcome your person with a smile and make some small talk before lunging into the crux of the debrief.

4. **Be Honest!** I hated it when the person debriefing me would "talk around" a subject and not about what I needed to work on. Give it straight! Depending on the person, direct feedback can be just one sentence or one example. Hit it quick, honest, and forthright. Trust me, they'll respect you MORE in the morning for it.

5. **Use the Goldilocks Principle for Targets (Keep Them Just Right)!** I like a good challenge but too many (or too few) can have an opposite effect on my long term performance. Keep performance targets "just right" when thinking about personal and professional goals. Ask your team member to give you a few, you contribute a few, come to a consensus on timelines and then develop the list of possible targets together. Targets without action steps to get there are like being on the right track but just sitting there (eventually you'll get run over).

6. **Give it like YOU'D want it.** We've all been there, done that and have the war wounds to prove it. We've gotten a great process of good feedback and some that were a bad process of terrible feedback, so we should know how we'd want to receive one. Think through the process as if you were giving it to yourself and treat the other person accordingly...fair, consistent, and factual. If you've gathered information through the year, had a history of clear and

honest communication, then the appraisal should be one that is productive and a true depiction of where things are.

These aren't the ONLY things needed to give a great performance review but they are **SIX** things that helped me make the most of the one's I did (and, like I said, I've done a lot of them). Keep it real and remember that you've been on the other side of the desk.

> ? **What's the BIG SECRET!?**
> A great performance appraisal starts a year in advance. Be prepared!

The Secret About Linking People To Value

"ARE YOU SERIOUS!?" I thought to myself as I got off the phone with my supervisor. This was the fourth time I had reworked this report - each time having had different directions, parameters, and requirements. Usually, I like things on my "done" list and not my "to do" list, but this time I felt a little different. I was frustrated, unmotivated, and yes, a little angry that I was going to have to work through this data again. This resulted in me having a conversation with myself that made me even angrier! At the peak of my self induced conversational frenzy, my supervisor walked in the door. I don't know if it was a look of surprise or death that I gave him as he stepped closer to me and began to speak but I know that it wasn't pleasant. In a very low, calm voice he said,

"Chip, I know that this has been frustrating, but let me tell you everything that's been going on with 'data call' (request for information) and why it's so important." He then explained all the information that hadn't been given to him at first but he also explained the value of what we were doing (in a nutshell, that the requirements we were justifying would, in the end, ensure others' safety). Immediately, my self talked changed from that of righteous indignation to that of an attitude of "how can I do more?" I learned an important lesson that day....VALUE MOTIVATES! Giving people the "why" of what they do creates value for them and, in turn, for the team. From that day forward I have worked to link people to value by valuing them in three ways.

First, I **value the person**. Each person brings something unique to the team. I have always envied my "Spock like" logical co-workers who approach each task as if they're about to perform brain surgery. That's not me and not in my "gift set. "What I do bring is passion for the task and creativity in getting it done. Those that have recognized this and valued it, motivated me to do more. As a supervisor, when I took the time to get to know my people, know their gifts and fit the job to their strengths, we were able to get more done as a team - each and every time.

Second, I **value the contribution**. Let's face it, we spend most of our waking hours at work or thinking about work. In the end, work has to mean more than just a paycheck. Each of us (including myself) wants to feel that we're making a difference in some way - that our contribution to the end result matters. The easiest way to let people know is, yes, to just tell them. Just as my supervisor communicated the importance of my contribution to the end result, I have worked to let others know the same. Telling a person is the first step - rewards are the second (a THANK YOU is a great start).

Third, I **value the relationship**. I've had very few jobs in my life where I woke up and thought, "HOLY CRAP!! I GET TO DO THIS TODAY!" For me, the joy in work has come partly from the type of work but mostly from the people I worked with. If we enjoyed each other, had fun, and were able to connect on a personal level, I was in my element. I am not saying that I have to be everyone's best friend. That's not possible. As leaders, we can create the type of environment where people flourish. This is done by sharing our time, our talents and our story. Anytime I've shared my story with another, it shared my humanity and encouraged them to do the same.

In today's world, we're all trying to do more with less and leverage what little we have left. Why not leverage the only real assets in our organization that matter - our people! If we want more value, it starts with relaying the value .By valuing the person, the contribution, and the relationship, your team will go further than you ever thought possible (and probably enjoy the trip a little more too).

? **What's the BIG SECRET!?**
If people know the "why" they will figure out the "how" to get it done!

The Secret About Pushing Your Idea Through

I sat there, nearly giddy as a young school girl, as the Admiral announced that nearly all of my wants for my division were about to be granted....funding, manpower, training. At that moment when my ideas became reality, I knew exactly how Dr. Frankenstein felt as he screamed, "IT'S ALIVE!! ALIVE I TELL YOU!!"

When you've put your heart and soul into an initiative, you can't help but feel some personal gratification when it comes to fruition. Even, if you don't get the credit. NOT GETTING THE CREDIT!? What is that about? When something is for the good of the team and/or the organization, it doesn't make a difference where the credit goes, as long as the initiative gets done. What I've found in 25 years of working in (and leading teams) is that ideas have to be set free and empowered to take on a life of their own. Especially if you need others to get the job done. Bringing life to an idea is more about letting go then holding on. Here are the strategies I use to make this happen:

Give It Up

Much like a mother bird tosses her chick out of the nest when it's ready, so must a good idea be tossed out to the team to be taken up, built on, and given wings. I've had a lot of GREAT ideas in my life. I'm not talking just good ideas...I am referring to fantastic ideas! Many of which I've held on to way too long. I fed them too long, held them too long, and let them stay around too long. So long, in fact, that (as the idea grew) it got too big for just one to manage but no one knew how to handle it except me (and it wasn't nearly as cute as it was when it was younger) - resulting in its possible demise (due to it being too hard to handle or my resenting it). Holding on too long stifles the overall growth, development, and progression of an idea. Giving an idea up gives it motion, momentum, and creativity - enabling it to move forward.

Talk It Up

If I have thrown an idea out of the nest and allowed it to take flight, I can't just abandon it. It may sound a bit cliché' or corny, but I must be the wing beneath its wings by talking it up at every opportunity. Even though I am proud, I can't run around saying, "Did you see my chick? Isn't she darling? Don't you just love her?" Instead, I must support from all sides by gently monitoring where it goes and whispering to all how it is doing, what support it needs, and how others can help the flight. This can be a difficult task. When pride runs too deep, egos run too high, and the wind that gets blown is too fierce, the idea will plummet to the earth and die. A gentle breeze beneath the wings is all that is needed to keep it airborne. Surround it with support.

Prop It Up

Barriers can get in the way of any ideas' new flight. It could be a strong gust from another direction or a huge tree right in the path of flight. The question is, what can be done to remove those barriers? Some may be removed through talking it up but some may take a little more savvy. It might require a compromise or to ask something to get out of the way. It might even require you take a chain saw and cut the tree out of the way. Think through the flight plan of this idea, prop it up, and provide as clear of a path as possible.

In a team, the life and flight of an idea might start with you. However, if you want to see it through, it's important to remember to initiate, don't smother. Give it up, talk it up, and prop it up - give the idea the support needed for it to fly. If it is a truly great idea, it will. If not, and you take it upon yourself to raise, you might end up with a overweight, 30 year old idea living with you that eats you out of house and home. The choice is yours! I think you'll find that many hands make for lighter work and greater results.

?

What's the BIG SECRET!?
Many hands make for lighter work and greater results!

The Secret About Nicknames

Growing up, my Dad had a nickname for everyone. I don't know he used them because he couldn't remember anyone's name or because he thought it was funny. Whatever the reason, if you knew him (and he liked you) you got assigned a name. At his work there was a Flopjaw, Leo, Goliath, and myriad of others. His naming wasn't just relegated to work; each of us kids had a name as well. My brothers were Buck, Beanhead, Doodle, and my sister was "Sis" (okay, not that imaginative but it was still a nickname). Either through nature or nurture, this "gift" for naming people was passed on to me. Regardless of where I worked or the position I held, I've named my co-workers. Never derogatory - but a positive reflection of the traits they radiated during their daily interaction with me. It made no difference if I was working with Sparky, Sprocket, or Sparkle, the result of my nicknaming was nearly always positive. Here's what it could do for you if you're willing to take the risk.

Force Reflection

If you are to come up with a really accurate and positive nickname for a co-worker, it takes time and reflection. You MUST take the time to really watch, learn, and get to know this person. This is never a bad thing - especially when you are focusing in on the good. We spend hours, days, and, yes, sometimes years, focusing in on the things that irritate us about others. Taking some time to focus in on the good can help us change our perceptions of that person and, in turn, appreciate them on a different level. If we change our perceptions, we can change our world!

Break Barriers

Once I would finalize a name (and, yes, it would sometimes take a few revisions to get it just right), I would start easing the person into their new name. Undoubtedly, the question would always arise, "Why are you calling me that?" This question would give me the perfect opportunity to ease into his or her positive traits. For instance, when working with Sprocket (who could be negative at times), I explained to her that she "Makes things go!" When I would call her Sprocket she would smile and I could see her spirit lift a bit. Here's the key: A nickname has to be positive and if the person doesn't like the name it can't be used.

Build Community

In a formal organization, we are quick to figure out who fits where and who does what. Once we have this down, we then start to know people as what they do versus who they are. Add some cubicles and email and you've got a nice, sterile environment where teamwork, productivity, and creativity wane. Nicknames add personality and are personable. They are a huge florescent splash of color on a flat white wall. When we know each other by more than title and/or job but as people, there's no limit to where we can go as an organization.

Do not feel as if this burden lies solely on you. Bring your team into the mix and ask them to help. Here are some possibilities for brainstorming at your next meeting to help each other come up with positive nicknames:

- Rap Names
- Disney Characters
- Greek Gods
- Western Icons

- Famous Explorers

The possibilities are endless and the rewards great when we work to know those around us, break barriers, and build community. Those are the organizations people want to be a part of - where they can flourish and progress is made! Oh, and my nicknames? I've been Chipper the Skipper, Golden Boy, The Professor, Pookey Bear, and one of the Wonder Twins. The best is the one coming from the master himself, my father, who just refers to me as "The Wiener."

What's the BIG SECRET!?
A well crafted nickname can help you connect with and motivate the team!

The Secret About Leaving a Legacy

When life is complete, what is the legacy you want to leave behind? One of policy, plans, procedures and rules? Do you want a to leave a legacy that represents your true self? At home, work, or play - if you want to leave a legacy that is of true value and that continues to be shared, then the answer is to tithe with others. I am not talking about giving 10% more than what you are giving right now. I am referring to sharing the 10% of yourself that makes you special. When we share our inner 10% with others, we pass that piece of ourselves on and can help others grow, develop, or move past a difficult time in their life. All the success I have ever enjoyed has been the result of another's tithe in me - all ordinary people become extraordinary because they take the time to invest the 10% that is personal, insightful, and sometimes painful (to share and to hear). Step up and start tithing today by being mindful of these principles.

Reflect

Having a PhD, tons of money, or a title is great, but the only requirement for you to tithe is having a willing spirit and a reflective mind. To be in that reflective state-of-mind when encountering issues, ask yourself: How can I help? What part of "me" can be of benefit to this person? Your tithe could come in the form of a personal story, an experience, a triumph, or even a tribulation. Regardless of its origin, it matters because it is a part of you. With a tithe, sometimes the smallest things have the largest impact. Always remember that each of us is special and has something to tithe.

Remove Distractions

We live in a busy world - cell phones, WiFi, and the continual bombardment of information can leave most so stressed they feel like they are diagonally parked in a parallel universe! To tithe, we need to take the time to connect on a human level - to get away from the distractions and meet others with warm eyes and an open heart. Only 7% of the words we use are important. The other 93% of a conversation comes from our body language, facial expressions, and how active we are in our ability to listen. Tithing can be as simple as turning off the cell phone, lending an ear, and just "being there."

Risk

Is there an element of risk in tithing? The answer is yes. There is the risk of your tithe being unwanted. There is the risk of your tithe falling on "deaf" ears. There may also be the risk of being hurt. The hardest part of tithing is making that first investment. No great thing was ever accomplished without battling with that element of risk. In life, there are people that do and people that wish they had done. Wouldn't you rather step out, take the risk of rejection and/or hurt and be of benefit to another than to have "wished" you had done something after the fact? I think the answer is clear - we should step up, step out, invest ourselves and take the risk.

Tithing is personal. It is a personal investment of your best 10% in others that goes beyond the boundaries of mentorship and coaching. It's about a covenant that we build with others in an attempt to make meaning of our experiences and provide value to others as we run the race of life. The tithe that we share lives on in those we invest in and, chances are, it will become part of their tithe in others. It's not a lot, it's only 10% - but that small investment will give returns that are much greater than we could ever expect. Don't hesitate, now is the time to reach out, connect, inspire, and make your investment in others through tithing. Now is also the time to thank those who have shared their tithes with you!

?	**What's the BIG SECRET!?** Policies and plans come and go. The only real legacy is the investment you make in others.

The Secret About Rewards

Is morale and productivity down with your team? Do team members have difficulty seeing the horizon because their gaze is fixed on the ground? Unlocking the door to team member motivation can appear to be a complex issue, but leaders should never underestimate the power of a "thank you." It articulates the value of each member's contribution to the team and says that he or she matters as a person. To open the doors and release the potential that each team member possesses, try these different keys:

Key #1: Reward People Differently. Just as performance differs between team members, so should the rewards you use. Reward the behavior you want to see! A smile, a "thank you," or a well-deserved "Great Job!" go a long way in keeping motivation high. Find out what motivates each team member and tailor your gratitude accordingly.

Key #2: Ignoring It Doesn't Make It Go Away. Dealing with a carrier? A carrier is that person that "carries" their negativity around like a disease and tries to infect the entire workplace? Emotions are contagious and that negativity can quickly spread through an entire department. Don't ignore it, address it – talk with your team member about what is going on and what you can do to help. Always remember to seek first to understand, then to be understood.

Key #3: Be Concise on What Warrants Rewards. Let's face it, clarity motivates! Team member empowerment and freedom come from knowing what needs to be done and what they get as a result. Don't keep rewards a secret and let people know the WIIFM (What's In It For Me).

Key #4: Be a Coach, Not a Critic. No team member finds the act of failing rewarding. Walk along side team members – help them along. Team loyalty and mutual respect emerge from a collective effort. Root for the home team and WIN!

Key #5: Build Them Up Publicly. Work to find people doing things right and let everyone know about it! Yell it from the rooftops! You'll be surprised how it motivates the whole team! Conversely, negative "publicity" should never be given in front of ANYONE - it impacts the overall work atmosphere and all team members end up getting punished.

Key #6: Be Fair. No team member should ever feel like doing a good job on your team is like peeing his or her pants in a dark suit (it gives them a warm feeling but no one notices). Keep the balance of rewards in check with open communication and an atmosphere of collaboration.

Key #7: Have Fun! Enjoying what you do is a reward that goes far beyond the bottom line. Forbes Magazine recently reported that 85% of Fortune 100 companies concern themselves with making sure that employees have fun and enjoy what they do. It boosts loyalty, retention, and productivity!

Don't be fooled, it takes time and effort to match the right key to the right door but it is worth the effort. When opened, you will not only have a team member that has higher morale and productivity, you will also have one that knows that you care.

> **What's the BIG SECRET!?**
> Rewards motivate and motivated people should be rewarded. Match the reward to the person.

The Secret About Managing The Remote Employee

I had worked tirelessly on my end of the month report to let my boss know what I had done. I didn't see him except for once or twice a year so I figured that he really needed to know what I was doing and how well I was doing it. I smugly sat back after I attached the file and hit the send button on my email. I knew that I was probably going to get a call commending me on what a great report I had done and how much he appreciated me being on the team. These were the thoughts that were going through my head as I sat there waiting, patiently for the phone to ring. One hour passed...nothing. Two hours...nothing. The day passed... nothing. After working hours were over, all I could figure from my lack of feed back was that he was (more than likely) showing it to everyone and asking their advice on how he could clone me and my awesomeness. The next day, week and month passed and I still heard nothing. I chalked it up to his being busy and that did not deter me from submitting an equally magnificent report at the end of the next month. Oddly, the same scenario prevailed. I expected a ticker tape parade and got a goose egg. To check to see if he even read my reports, the next month I submitted the same report as the month before and, yes, I got nothing. That was the report I submitted for the next two years (without any edits).

As a remote employee, I felt a little discouraged. Since the basic numbers that I was judged by were okay, my boss let me be. As an employee that likes autonomy and kingdom building, this worked fine by me, however, that's not the case with all. I could have very easily joined the ranks of the unmotivated, unengaged, and misunderstood.

Are you managing a remote employee and having trouble keeping them engaged or feeling as if they are part of the team? I think there are 4 sins leaders commit with remote employees. Here they are and how you can combat them:

SIN #1: NOT HERE, NOT AS IMPORTANT

We are busy and nothing is as important as right now. Most things had to have been done yesterday and all we have is right now to get them done. If they don't get done right now then yesterday's priorities quickly become tomorrow's disciplinary items. The result is that we slip on placing an equal importance on the work that's done outside of our right now.

What can you do? Make a schedule to talk to your remote employee and keep it (regardless of the "right now" priorities). I suggest two types of meetings. One to cover priorities and another each week to just "check in" on how they are and to connect. Both will bring great returns.

SIN #2: NOT AROUND, NOT INFORMED

There's a big difference between real time and remote time. Real time provides the opportunity to pick up on cues, have casual conversations and be in "the know" on most things that happen. Remote time does not. For instance, if you have a weekly teleconference that includes your remote employees, the last time they were in "real time" with you was last week. A million different things have been said since then in real time that may have changed the way things are done and/or perceived. Your remote employee (living in remote time) has not been privy to any of this.

What can you do? Bridge the gap by keeping track of what's going on in real time and informing your remote employee. You can do this during your normally scheduled talks or by sending out a weekly recap to EVERYONE (not just the remote employee). This will encourage exchange between the two types of team members.

SIN #3: NOT AROUND, NOT INCLUDED

I love potluck Tuesdays, Wacky Wednesdays, Donut Thursdays and casual everyday. These, along with the trials and work we face together, are the building blocks of how we build a team and create esprit de corps. It's also, unfortunately, how remote workers can feel left out. They didn't hear about what Jim did at the copier or how Sally's son won the junior chili cook off because they had Donut Thursday by themselves.

What can you do? You can include them! Phone or Skype them in for the potluck or other work event! Ask them what they made and how it tastes. Encourage others to bring them into the fold by doing the same and using instant messaging to make them feel a part of the team. Better yet, PLAN a monthly get together in person for EVERYONE. Don't leave it to chance that they'll be talked to. Structure it so that they are.

SIN #4: NOT PRESENT, NOT ACKNOWLEDGED

Leaders can negate the power of their saying a casual "good job" to someone or even just paying attention to what's going on with their team members. Good leaders pass along that acknowledgement on a consistent basis throughout their work day and know their employees. Further, they set clear expectations.

What can you do? Great leaders remember to show the same courtesy with the virtual employee. Set the expectation, keep track of what is going on and acknowledge the contribution of the remote employee EVERY time you talk. Working for you should never feel to a remote employee like peeing their pants in a dark suit (it gives them warm feeling but nobody notices).

The truth is that it takes more effort to effectively lead a remote employee. I, as a remote employee, stayed engaged because that is in my nature. Even so, I still felt a little discouraged when I didn't feel as if I was important and that my contribution wasn't valued. At our core, everyone wants to feel like they are a part of something and that our contribution is valued. Remote employee engagement starts with leader engagement. Don't get sucked into committing these four sins. REPENT and get engaged!

> ?
>
> **What's the BIG SECRET!?**
> Remote employee engagement STARTS with leader engagement.

The Secret About The Secret

Like I stated at the beginning of this book, there are no secrets or quick fixes in leading people. There are many lessons I had to learn the hard way in trying to move my teams forward and lead the right way. The right way, in many ways, is your way. Each of us must find our unique leadership style and lead from the heart of it. For me, that started as a plump child. Those are my roots. It helped me lead with empathy and humor. Yours may be different.

I hope you've gotten value from the strategies I've shared in this book. Continue to pick this book up, read it, reflect on it and act. Not everything you do as a leader will be perfect. Mistakes will be made...that's part of the process. That is okay and expected! That's human nature! The important thing is that you continue to learn, grow and act. Leading is about action, not intent.

About Lieutenant Commander Chip Lutz

United States Navy, Retired

Chip Lutz is a leader who's been there, done that, and has the uniform to prove it! He works with leaders who want to lead better, get more done, and leave a legacy.

A retired Naval Officer, under his command as Commanding Officer of two different Naval facilities, both his teams received national recognition for setting new standards of service while maintaining high morale and high retention among team members. He also knows about meeting critical objectives during stressful conditions – having served as the Director of Security for Naval District Washington, DC during September 11th, 2001 – where he was responsible for the safety and security of 25 thousand people on 9 different Naval installations in the National Capital Region.

He is the husband to the fair maiden Gwen, father of 4, visiting professor, author, friend to his dog Oliver – does dishes, cooks, does laundry...but hates to fold whites.

You can get more information about his work at www.unconventionalleader.com.